WORLD GAMES
AND
RECIPES

THE WORLD ASSOCIATION OF
GIRL GUIDES
AND GIRL SCOUTS

World Bureau, Olave Centre, 12c Lyndhurst Road, London NW3 5PQ, England

The recipes in this book have been collected from WAGGGS members worldwide, and therefore the World Association of Girl Guides and Girl Scouts cannot take responsibility for their accuracy.

For younger members, the supervision of an adult is recommended.

First Edition 1979
Reprinted 1981
Reprinted 1984
Second Edition 1988
Reprinted March 1994
Reprinted October 1994
ISBN 0 900827 43 2

The first edition of this book was produced
by courtesy of Nestlé S.A., Vevey, Switzerland

ACKNOWLEDGEMENTS

The recipes given for
Locro de Pipap, Halta,
Kesakeitlo,
Jamaica Pepperpot,
Green Bananas, Guacamole,
Erwtensoup,
Fish Loaf, Adobo and Jollof Rice
are reprinted by kind permission
of the United Nations
Women's Guild
and their members in
Ecuador, Egypt, Finland, Jamaica,
Kenya, Mexico, Netherlands,
Norway, Philippines and
Sierra Leone.
All games
and all other recipes in this book
come from WAGGGS National
Associations.

CONVERSION TABLES

OVEN TEMPERATURES

GAS MARK	°F	°C
¼	225	110
½	250	130
1	275	140
2	300	150
3	325	170
4	350	180
5	375	190
6	400	200
7	425	220
8	450	230
9	475	240

VOLUME

2 fl oz	55 ml
3 fl oz	75 ml
¼ pint	150 ml
1 cup	236 ml
8 fl oz	236 ml
½ pint	275 ml
1 pint	570 ml
18 fl oz	½ litre
1¾ pints	1 litre
½ tsp	2.5 ml
1 tsp	5 ml
1 dsp	10 ml
1 tbs	15 ml

WEIGHT

½ oz	10g
1 oz	25g
1½ oz	40g
2 oz	50g
2½ oz	60g
3 oz	75g
4 oz	110g
4½ oz	125g
5 oz	150g
6 oz	175g
7 oz	200g
8 oz	225g
9 oz	250g
10 oz	275g
12 oz	350g
1 lb	450g
1½ lb	700g
2 lb	900g
2.2 lb	1kg

CONTENTS

Wherever you live, whatever your eating habits, whether you are very young or very old, you should know a little about *how* to eat. This little book we have made for you has recipes from many different countries, with different kinds of ingredients. They are all more or less healthy — 'nutritious', but the important thing is to make sure that the *combination* of what you eat during the whole day is *well balanced.*

The basic four

This diagram shows you the four most important kinds of food for a nutritious diet.

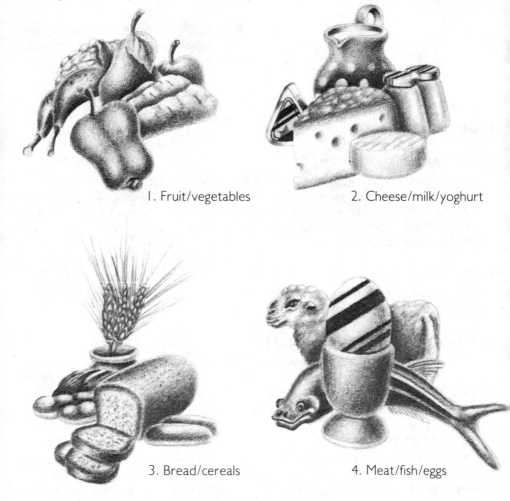

1. Fruit/vegetables

2. Cheese/milk/yoghurt

3. Bread/cereals

4. Meat/fish/eggs

Try to eat a little of all these, every day.

It is better to eat small meals at intervals throughout the whole day rather than one large meal. The ideal is for breakfast to give us 20-25% of our daily needs and lunch and dinner each 30%. In between meals could give the other 15-20%.

1 Too many of us do not eat enough *fruit and vegetables*. Fruit and vegetables give us Vitamins A and C, minerals, good carbohydrate and fibre.

2 *Milk and milk products*, such as cheese and yoghurt, give us protein, calcium and Vitamin B.

3 *Cereals and bread* give us Vitamin B, iron, and, also important carbohydrates and fibre.

4 *Meat, fish and eggs* give us protein. They also supply important minerals and some vitamins.

A nutritional glossary

Proteins: the body's building stones

Proteins are essential. They can't be stored in the body as are fat and carbohydrates, and so we should eat some protein every day. Proteins are the body's 'building stones' and are therefore especially important for children and young people, who are still growing. Proteins are found in animal foods such as fish, meat, eggs, milk and milk products, as well as in some pulses and vegetables.

Fats: both good and bad

Fats give energy, twice as much per gramme as proteins and carbohydrates. However, it is not good to eat too much fat.

Carbohydrates: good — but watch the sugar!

Carbohydrates (sugar, starch and cellulose) mostly give us energy. *Sugar is the quickest energy giver, but it doesn't contain any good nutrients.* Starch, which we get from bread, cereals and vegetables, is the best source of carbohydrate. Cellulose, which is found in all vegetables, aids digestion because it supplies roughage.

Minerals: the tools for the body

Minerals do not give us any energy, but have other important uses. We need calcium and phosphorus to build bones and teeth, iron to help the body to make red blood cells. Women especially should make sure they have enough iron in their diet, because it is easy to become anaemic — not having enough red blood cells. Liver, meat, bread, spinach and other green vegetables are all good sources of iron.

Vitamins: important for the metabolism

The many different vitamins are present in small amounts in most of our food. We usually get all vitamins we need, if we eat a variety of sensible foods.

Water

The body is made of up to 70 % water and to be healthy this level has to be maintained. As we lose about 2 litres of water each day, we should also take in the same amount. We do this through drinking, but also through the food we eat.

Energy — what is it?

The food we eat is used to give the energy we need to drive the body, as an engine burns petrol. Different foods can give quite different amounts of energy. We measure the energy from protein, fat and carbohydates in kilo calories — 'kcal', or in joules — 'j'. One kcal is the same as 4.2 kj (kilo joule).

Fibres

Fibres are the non-digestible parts of food, found in vegetables and cereals. Although the body can't use fibre for energy or to build tissue it is necessary to help get rid of waste.

Food and Exercise

Do remember that it is just as important to be active and take regular exercise as to eat well. This book has games in it as well as recipes, and after you have cooked and eaten the meals in the recipes you can give your body some of the exercise it needs by playing the games!

∧ Girl Guides prepare a meal at camp in Yemen

∨ Girl Guides and Girl Scouts sing together at Our Cabaña

< On camp in the Netherlands

∨ Visually impaired Brownies in Kenya
enjoy a dancing game

< Brownies spend a day painting in Australia

∨ Girl Scouts in the Philippines prepare a camp meal

∧ *Obstacles and challenges in Norway*
∨ *Volleyball in the United Arab Emirates*

15

∧ Guides participate in a national jamboree in India

< Meal-time at Sangam

< Brownies demonstrat
a street market in
Oman

V Recreational day cam
at Our Cabaña

↖ *Girl Scouts in Japan walk the rope*
↙ *Absailing in Nepal*

∧ A traditional game in Bahrain

< Norwegian Girl Scouts enjoy a cookery lesson

El Gato y el Ratón —
'Cat and Mouse' (Brownie game)

Players join hands in a circle. One player, 'Mouse', stands inside the circle. Another, 'Cat', stands outside the circle facing Mouse.

Cat: Mouse, what are you doing in my vineyard?
Mouse: Eating grapes.
(Cat holds her hand out towards Mouse)
Cat: Give me some.

(Mouse reaches through the circle and pretends to put some grapes into Cat's hands.)

Mouse: Here they are.
Cat: Give me more.

This may be repeated as often as Mouse wishes to answer: Here they are. It goes on:

Cat: Give me more.
Mouse: No!
Cat: I'll catch you.
Mouse: If you can.

Mouse runs and Cat chases her. The players in the circle try to protect Mouse. If Cat enters the circle by going under two joined hands they let Mouse out. If both Cat and Mouse are outside the circle they help Mouse enter. When Cat catches Mouse, two other players take their places and play begins again.

Fill the Bottle Race

Played in teams. Each team, standing in a line, has a pail of water at one end and an empty bottle and teaspoon at the other. The water from the bucket is transferred by the spoon, passed from one player to another along the line. The first team to fill the bottle to a fixed mark within a time limit wins.

Gelignite sticks (Patrol or Six game)

Each member of the Patrol or the Six is given a 'gelignite stick' — a rolled-up magazine or newspaper secured by sellotape or string.

On the word 'go' they try to get rid of a gelignite stick by tapping a girl from another Patrol or Six with it. She must then take the stick and quickly try to get rid of it in the same way.

The game continues until a given signal when everybody returns to their own Six or Patrol and counts the number of sticks held by their group. The group holding the LOWEST number is the winner.

Perhaps it should be stressed that the girls 'tap' each other!

Dampers

450 g flour
125 g powdered milk
10 g sugar
salt
125 g butter or margarine
375 ml cold water

Tasty additions

handful mixed fruit or sultanas
125 g grated cheese (leave out sugar)

1 Mix together flour, powdered milk, sugar and salt.

2 Rub in butter until mixture has the appearance of rice grains, then add water. Mix to a stiff consistency and knead well.

3 Wind round a clean stick and cook in fire until brown and well-risen. Eat with butter or jam.

Glen Elgin Carrot Salad

900 g young carrots
juice of 4 small oranges
sugar

Dressing:

3 tbs olive oil
1 tbs white wine vinegar
mint leaves
1 clove garlic, crushed

Garnish:

chives
nasturtium leaves
hibiscus blossom

1 Peel and grate carrots into a salad bowl, add orange juice and sprinkle with sugar.

2 Make dressing with garlic, olive oil, white wine vinegar, crushed mint leaves and salt. Mix thoroughly.

3 Pour dressing over carrots: mix well. Garnish with chopped chives and nasturtium leaves and decorate the dish with hibiscus blossom.

Simplicity Chocolate Cake

250 g flour
250 g sugar
30 g cocoa
45 g butter, melted
2 eggs
25 ml milk
2.5 ml almond essence (optional)

Icing:

260 g icing sugar
30 g cocoa
75 g margarine
50 ml water

walnuts for decoration

1 Put all ingredients into a large basin and pour melted butter on top. Beat really hard for 3 minutes.

2 Bake in a greased tin in moderate (350°F, 180°C) oven for about 30 minutes.

3 Make icing by mixing icing sugar, cocoa, margarine and water until light and fluffy.

4 Allow cake to cool, ice and decorate with walnuts. For variety, split this cake in two and fill with the icing.

AUSTRIA

Wiener Schnitzel

5 veal escalopes
2 eggs
salt, pepper, savory, thyme
flour
breadcrumbs
butter for frying

Garnish:

lemon slices

1 Beat eggs with herbs and seasoning.

2 Pound veal until very thin, then dust in flour. Dip each escalope in egg mixture and coat with breadcrumbs.

3 Heat two or three tablespoons of butter in frying pan and fry veal till crisp. Garnish with slices of lemon.

BELGIUM

Passwords

A game to play when waiting for the train or bus to camp.

All the girls stand in a straight line. The last in line decides on a word. With her finger she 'writes' the first letter of the word on the back of the girl immediately in front of her. The second girl then does the same on the back of the girl in front of her, and so on until the front of the line is reached. Each letter of the word is passed on in the same way. The girl at the front of the line has to say what the word is.·

It is surprising how different the word can turn out to be!

Omelettes at Camp

I egg,
I thick slice from
a French loaf
each.

1 Make a hollow in the bread and place the remaining crust on a flat stone.

2 Break an egg, beat it and pour it into the hollow.

3 Place — on the stone — in embers of fire until the egg is cooked.

_____ **BRAZIL** _____

Zoo Game (Brownie game)

Play this game in a big room or a garden.

Each Six chooses a different animal which makes a definite noise. Every Brownie is blindfolded and everyone scatters. At a signal from Brown Owl, every Brownie moves round making her own animal noise. Each Six has to gather together by sound alone.

The first one complete in a straight line is the winner.

Catch the Broom (Guide game)

This game can be played indoors or out.

Players form a circle and each girl is given a number. One player is chosen to stand in the middle of the circle, holding a broom.

She calls out a number and then lets go of the broom. The player whose number is called must run and catch the broom before it falls on the floor.

If she catches the broom, she replaces the player in the middle of the circle. If she does not catch it, she is out of the game.

Play continues in the same way but if the player in the middle calls out the number of a player who is already out, she is also out of the game and must be replaced by another player. The game ends when only one girl is left.

Camouflage

This is best played in a place where there is good cover.

The leader stands in an open central spot and covers her eyes for five minutes. During this time the players all hide, but they must be able to see the leader from their hiding place. A signal is given and the leader opens her eyes. Within a pre-arranged time limit, and without moving from her place (although she may turn around), she must see how many hiders she can spot.

This is excellent practice in keeping still.

Fireflies (Night game)

This is played in two teams, A and B. Each member of team A has a flashlight and is a firefly. They are then given several minutes to hide within whatever boundaries are set for the game.

When the leader blows her whistle the fireflies must switch on their flashlights for a few seconds and team B must try to capture them. A good means of capture is to have a strip of fabric or coloured plastic (stuck in team A's belts) which must be taken. The leader should blow the 'flashlights on' signal at regular intervals and the fireflies should keep changing position.

At the end of ten or fifteen minutes the teams can change places. The team with the most captives wins.

International Shopping

Played in Patrols grouped round the room. The game leader has a list of items that could be bought in a store.

One person from each Patrol, the shopper, comes to the leader. All are given the same items. They return to their Patrol, which is the 'shop' and mime what they want to buy. The first Patrol to guess correctly wins and the game is repeated with new 'shoppers'.

Super Baked Apples

I apple each
butterscotch chips
marshmallows
foil

1 Remove core of apple carefully and set it on a square of foil, then fill cavity with butterscotch and marshmallows.

2 Wrap apple in foil and bake in hot coals until soft (10-30 minutes).

Sloppy Joes

450 g minced beef
tomato or chicken soup (or both)
ketchup
prepared mustard
rolls or French bread

1 Brown the mince in a frying pan (pour off excess fat).

2 Add soup(s), ketchup and mustard. Heat through.

3 Serve on split hamburger rolls or slices of French bread.

Foil Dinner (serves 4)

I chicken, quartered (or 4 chicken joints)
2 medium zucchini (courgettes) sliced
I green pepper, cut in strips
I medium onion, sliced thinly
I 275 g (large) can mushrooms
I 400 g can tomatoes
salt and pepper
dried oregano
dried basil
185 g rice
Parmesan cheese, grated

1 Place 30 g rice in centre of each of 4 squares of heavy duty foil.

2 Season chicken and place on top of rice.

3 Drain mushrooms (reserving liquid), divide mushrooms, zucchini, green pepper and onion into four and place over each piece of chicken.

4 Mix tomatoes, reserved mushroom liquid, pepper, oregano and basil. Spoon mixture over vegetables and chicken.

5 Fold foil over food and seal tightly. Place over coals, and cook until done, turning occasionally — about 30 minutes.

6 Sprinkle with Parmesan cheese before serving.

Lame Chicken (Brownie game)

Each Six has 10 sticks which are placed 10-12 inches (25-30 cm) apart like the rungs of a ladder-one row in front of each Six and a short distance away from the Brownies. (Shoes could be used instead of sticks.)

The first Brownie in each Six is the 'lame chicken' and she must hop over the sticks without touching them. After hopping over the last stick, she picks it up and hops back with it, placing it at the beginning. She is out of the game if both feet touch the ground or she touches a stick with her feet when hopping.

The next Brownie then becomes the 'lame chicken' and the game continues in the same way until they have all had a turn.

COLOMBIA

Juan Palmada — 'Johnny Clap-Hands' (Brownie game)

The Brownies make a circle, leaving one empty place in it. Two Brownies stand by the space, back to back, outside the circle.

At a signal these two run in opposite directions around the circle. When they meet, each jumps into the air and claps her hands over her head. Then they continue running to see which one can reach the empty space first.

The leader chooses another girl to take her place and the game continues.

Anyone who loses three times must pay a forfeit chosen by the pack.
(The forfeits should be of wide variety: recite a verse, turn a somersault, find three round pebbles, etc.)

Tomato and egg open sandwiches
(serves 6)

6 slices bread
4 eggs
4 small tomatoes
2 small onions
butter

Garnish:

lettuce leaves
cress

1 Hard boil eggs, wash vegetables, peel and slice onions, chop cress.

2 Butter the slices of bread and place alternate layers of sliced egg, tomatoes and onions on them.

3 Garnish with lettuce leaves and cress.

Brune Lager (This is a delicious spicy biscuit)

1 kg flour
1/2 kg sugar
1/4 kg syrup
1/2 kg butter or margarine
3 tsp bicarbonate of soda
4 tsp ground cinnamon
1 tsp ground cloves
125 g chopped almonds (optional)

1 Mix together sugar, butter, syrup: heat gently. Add bicarb mixed in little water.

2 Take off the heat, add spices (and almonds if liked), and fold in flour.

3 Form mixture into a roll (like a sausage!) and leave overnight.

4 Cut into thin slices and bake in a moderate/hot (425°F, 225°C) oven until a medium dark-brown colour.

Blackcurrant Muffins

250 g sifted flour
2 tsp baking powder
60 g butter
85 g sugar
2 eggs
500 g blackcurrants
milk
salt

1 Mix butter and sugar until creamy, gradually add beaten eggs and mix well.

2 Sift together and add flour, baking powder, salt. Gradually mix in milk until all lumps disappear.

3 Add blackcurrants.

4 Bake in greased cake tins at 400°F/ 200°C about 10 minutes (Makes 15 muffins).

Locro de Pipap (Potato Soup)

6 medium potatoes, peeled and cubed
2 green onions, finely chopped
vegetable oil
250 g Cheddar cheese, grated
2 eggs
250 ml milk
salt
paprika
1 1/2 litres water

Garnish:

1 avocado, cut in slices
lettuce leaves
chilli sauce (optional)

1 Put 250 ml water into a pan, add vegetable oil, finely chopped onion and seasoning: boil until onion is transparent.

2 Add rest of water and potatoes, cook until potatoes are done.

3 Allow to cool slightly, then add cheese and well-beaten eggs. Return to heat and warm through.

4 Serve garnished with lettuce and avocado (if liked). Add dash of hot chilli sauce.

EGYPT

Halta (serves 4)

225 g liver
500 g rice
2 onions, chopped
225 g sultanas
125 g cashew nuts
1 litre hot water
60 ml oil
salt

1 Cut up and fry liver. Fry cashew nuts. Take off heat and keep warm.

2 Fry rice and onion until brown. Add salt and hot water, simmer over low heat until rice is cooked (about 25 minutes).

3 Add nuts, liver and sultanas to rice mixture.

EL SALVADOR

Rice Pudding

450 g rice
225 g sugar
750 ml milk
1/2 tsp vanilla essence
1 small stick of cinnamon
raisins to decorate
flour and water if necessary

1 Soak rice in milk for at least 30 minutes.

2 Add sugar and cinnamon and cook over moderate heat until the rice is soft. (If a thicker consistency is liked, add 2 teaspoonsful of flour dissolved in water.)

3 Remove from heat and add vanilla essence and raisins.

Pineapple Coconut Pie

2 cups of milk
2½ cups of plain flour
2 cups of white sugar
3 eggs, separated
2 tbs lemon juice
2 tbs butter

1½ cups of grated, cooked pineapple
(or tinned)
1 cup of grated coconut (or dessicated)
1 pinch of salt
2 tbs margarine
2 tbs lard

Rub together the margarine, lard and two cups of flour until the mixture resembles fine bread-crumbs. Add water gradually until the mixture holds together. Grease an 8″ pie dish. Roll out pastry to line pie dish. Line pastry case with baking beans or bread. Bake pastry case at gas mark 7 for 10 minutes then remove baking beans or bread, lower temperature to gas mark 6 and cook for a further 10 minutes.

Melt butter over a low heat and add remaining flour, stirring to form a smooth paste. Gradually add milk stirring constantly. Add a cup of sugar and a pinch of salt. Stir until mixture thickens. Add beaten eggs and cook for three minutes. Mix lemon juice, pineapple and coconut together and add to mixture. Pour into pastry case. Allow to cool.

Beat together egg whites and two tablespoons of water until the mixture is stiff. Add half a cup of sugar and beat until the mixture forms peaks. Using a metal spoon, fold in remainder of sugar. Spoon mixture over filling and bake in oven for 10 minutes, gas mark 5.

Kesakeitlo (Summer Soup) (serves 4-6)

1 carrot, sliced
60 g green peas
1 small cauliflower, cut into pieces
5 small potatoes
few sliced spinach leaves
60 cl water
65 cl hot milk
seasoning

Garnish

finely chopped parsley
butter

1 Cook potatoes, carrot and peas in boiling salted water.

2 Add hot milk, spinach and cauliflower. Simmer for 20 minutes or until vegetables are soft.

3 Before serving dot with butter and garnish with finely chopped parsley.

Acrostiche

An outdoor game, played in teams.

Each team is given a word of a dozen letters to spell. The players have to find things beginning with each of the letters of their word.

The winning team is the one which finds all the objects in the shortest time, or the most objects in a given time.

Les portraits robots — 'Sketch Impressions'

A game for getting to know one another (all ages).

The game leader has one card for each girl with her name on.

The leader shuffles and deals the cards, so that every girl has one. Each player writes on the card a description of the person whose name is on the card. When they have finished the leader collects the cards and begins to read the description, without the name. Those who think they know the name may shout it out but the leader does not stop until the correct answer has been given. The game continues until all cards have been read.

Tuna fish rice salad (serves 4)

I can (400 g) tuna fish
200 g rice
black olives
radishes
tomatoes
green peppers

Dressing:
I tbs oil
2 tbs wine vinegar
dry mustard
herbs

Garnish:
lettuce

1 Boil rice.

2 Make dressing and mix into rice.

3 Add flaked tuna fish, some black olives, chopped radishes, quartered tomatoes and chopped green peppers.

4 Garnish with lettuce.

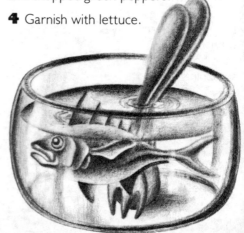

Provençale Tomatoes

Tomatoes
Garlic
Parsley, thyme, rosemary or oregano
Butter or margarine if liked.

1 Cut the tomatoes in half; add a small knob of butter or margarine.

2 Grill under flame for 2 minutes each side

3 Top with a layer of herbs and chopped garlic.

4 Cover with foil and allow to cook gently for 5-10 minutes.

GERMANY

How Will It End? (a drawing game)

Place a large sheet of drawing paper on the wall. The first player thinks of a picture and begins to draw it with a few lines. The next player adds to the drawing, then the next and so on. Each player must change the drawing each time, so that it looks as different as possible. Compare the final drawing with what the first player thought of!

Himmel und Erde (heaven and earth)

1.5kg potatoes
700 g apples
150 g bacon
100 g onions
500 cl water
sugar
vinegar
salt
oil for frying

1 Peel and slice potatoes into strips: peel and quarter apples.

2 Put potatoes in a saucepan with a little salt, sugar and water.

3 Bring to boil, then simmer on low heat until soft. Add the apples for the last 5 minutes.

4 Take off heat, adjust seasoning, add vinegar.

5 Cut bacon into strips and brown in frying pan with sliced onions.

6 Serve apple and potato mixture with bacon and onion poured on top.

Kwa-Kwa — 'The Blind Crow'

The players form a circle. One girl remains in the middle of the circle — she is the blind crow. She is blindfolded and while she moves slowly around flapping her arms like wings the players in the circle all change places. The first one to be touched by the 'wings' then becomes the blind crow.

GREECE

Birds — Giants — Dwarfs (Brownie game)

The Brownies stand in a circle with one Brownie in the middle. She gives the orders: 'Birds'; 'Giants'; 'Dwarfs'; or 'Wicked Witch'.

When the order is 'Birds' the Brownies pretend to fly. They walk tall for 'Giants', and creep low for 'Dwarfs'. When the Brownie in the middle calls 'Wicked Witch', all the Brownies run away to a place which has been chosen beforehand.

The Brownie from the middle chases them, and the first one to be caught gives the orders next.

The Puppet (Brownie game)

One Brownie is chosen to be the Mother and she stands outside a circle of Brownies, all sitting cross-legged.

A 'puppet doll' — made from a handkerchief or a scarf — is passed quickly round the circle in either direction so that the 'Mother' cannot catch it, as she runs round the outside of the circle.

When she does at last get 'her child' she changes places with the Brownie who was holding it at the time.

GUYANA

Steamed Fish

2-3 fillets fish
15 g chopped shallots and onions
butter
salt and pepper
lime juice to taste

1 Clean and season fish.

2 Bring a pan of water to the boil and grease a baking plate.

3 Place fish on plate with small dab of butter and add shallots and onions; squeeze lime juice over.

Garnish:
limes/tomatoes

4 Cover plate and steam over boiling water — allow 25 minutes for small pieces of fish *or* 15 minutes per pound, plus 15 minutes, for a large fish.

5 Garnish with slices of limes or tomatoes.

Fish Pie

225 g cooked fish
450 g cooked root vegetable
e.g.yam/potato
1 tbs chopped celery, shallot and onion
margarine
30 ml milk
salt and pepper

1 Skin, bone and flake fish, mix with milk, salt, pepper, celery, shallots and onion, and place in greased pie dish.

2 Mash cooked yam/potato with margarine and a little milk and place on top of fish.

3 Bake in hot (400°F/200°C) oven until brown (about 30 minutes).

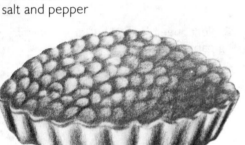

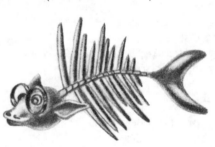

ICELAND

The Egg Game (Brownie game)

All the Brownies stand in a circle facing inwards with their legs apart.

One Brownie has a ball about the size of a basket ball and she starts the game by trying to roll the ball through someone's legs. No-one may put her feet together so each Brownie must try to stop the ball with her hands. A Brownie who stops the ball with her hands may try to roll it between someone else's legs but she may not move from her place in the circle.

If the ball does go through someone's legs that Brownie is out. The game continues until only one player is left.

Pass On

For this game a bag containing slips of paper numbered one to ten is needed.

Players stand or sit in a circle and pass the bag to each other. The game leader blows a whistle and the Guide holding the bag at that time takes out one slip of paper and calls out the number. She must then recite the part of the Girl Guide Law which has that number.

Players continue passing the bag round the circle until all numbers have been picked and all the Law recited.

Banana Chapati

500 g wheat flour
1 tsp baking powder
250 g sugar
2 eggs
125 ml milk
250 g mashed banana
salt to taste
125 g dry fruit (optional)
125 g ghee or clarified butter

1 Mix all ingredients well, adding more milk if necessary.

2 Heat ghee/clarified butter in heavy frying pan or on griddle.

3 Fry large spoonfuls of mixture on both sides until brown.

Vadai

500 g sorghum/durra flour
1 tsp baking powder
250 g chopped onion
2 green chillies
pinch of ginger
curry leaves (if available)
ground pepper
salt
oil for frying

1 Mix flour well with baking powder.

2 Add onion, chillies, pepper, ginger, curry leaves and salt to taste.

3 Mix with water to a thick batter.

4 Fry in oil until crisp.

IRELAND

Colcannon

1 lb kale
1 lb potatoes

salt and pepper
1 oz butter

Boil kale and potatoes separately. A sliced onion may be added to the potatoes. Mash the potatoes, add butter and seasoning. Chop kale and add to potatoes. Mix well. Serve hot.

Potato Cakes

2 cups freshly mashed potatoes
2 tbs butter or bacon fat
4 tbs plain flour

Mash the potatoes well and add fat. Work in the flour. Roll potato mixture out until it is ½″ (25mm) thick and cut into shapes. Fry in a greased pan for 3 minutes on either side. Serve with bacon or sausages.

Potato cakes can also be cooked on a dry griddle or in the oven and may then be served with butter and jam.

_____ **ISRAEL** _____

Falafel (makes about 75)

450 g chick peas
60 g cracked wheat
2 tsp baking powder
2 slices bread
4 crushed garlic cloves
chopped parsley
salt
ground cumin
coriander
paprika
black pepper
30 g breadcrumbs
oil for frying

1 Soak chick peas overnight in plenty of water with baking powder. Drain well.

2 Soak wheat in hot water for about 20 minutes.

3 Grind chick peas twice (or chop finely) and place in bowl.

4 Wet bread under running water. Squeeze out excess water and mix thoroughly into chick peas with garlic and parsley.

5 Add soaked wheat, seasoning and breadcrumbs. Mix thoroughly, then allow to stand for 15 minutes.

6 Pinch off pieces of the mixture and roll into 1 inch balls. Deep fry in oil, a few at a time, until golden brown. Remove from fat with slotted spoon, drain on paper towels.

7 Serve while hot on toothpicks or in the pocket of a pitta bread.

Risotto con Scampi (Rice with Shrimps)

450 g shrimps, shelled and cleaned (if using frozen shrimps, thaw 1 hour at room
temperature)
500 g long grain rice
1 crushed clove garlic
500 ml tomato sauce (16 to 17 oz can)
2 beef bouillon cubes or 2 serving-size
envelopes dry mix beef broth
1 litre hot water
60 g margarine or butter
60 ml cooking oil
salt and pepper to taste
fresh parsley, finely chopped
grated Parmesan cheese

1 Cook garlic in margarine/butter and oil
at medium heat until light brown, then
remove garlic.

2 Add rice and cook until golden brown,
stirring continuously. Lower heat.

3 Heat tomato sauce with beef cubes or
mix, and add to rice gradually, stirring continuously.

4 Add hot water, salt and pepper. Stir
thoroughly, cover and simmer over very
slow heat for 20 minutes, stirring occasionally. If necessary add a little more hot
water. Rice should be soft but not mushy.

5 Add shrimps and parsley, stir, cover
pan and cook for a further 5 minutes only.
Serve with cheese sprinkled generously on
top.

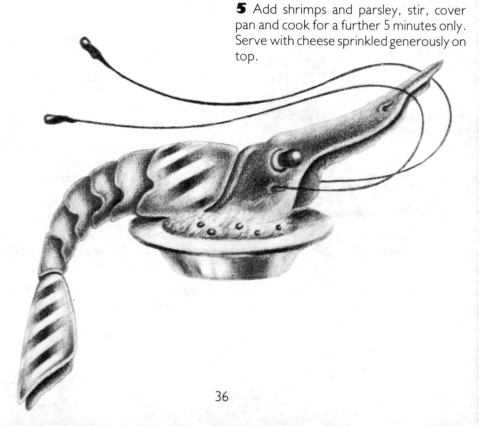

JAMAICA

Jamaica Pepperpot (serves 8)

100 g beef — cubed
450 g minced beef
900 g cabbage *or* kale
12 okra
2 onions
2 green onions, sliced
250 g fresh or dried coconut
1 litre water
salt
cayenne pepper
thyme

1 Wash cabbage/kale, cutting away discoloured or tough parts; cut into large pieces and place in pan with cubed beef, minced beef, okra, onions, coconut and water. Bring to boil and cook over low heat for 1 hour.

2 Remove cabbage/kale and okra. Sieve and return to pan.

3 Add salt, cayenne pepper, thyme, green onions, and cook a further 15 minutes or until meat is tender.

JAPAN

Jan-Ken-Pon (Brownie game)

Two Brownies face each other with hands behind them. Together they say, 'Jan-Ken-Pon'. On 'Pon' both bring their hands forward to represent stone, paper or scissors. A clenched fist is stone, an open hand is paper and scissors are made by holding out a hand with index and middle finger extended.

Stone beats scissors because it blunts them: scissors beats paper because they can cut it: the paper beats the stone because it can wrap it.

Each time a Brownie wins, she gains a point for her Six.

KENYA

Green Bananas (serves 6-8)

450 g beef, cut in chunks
450 g green bananas (plantains)
2 medium onions, sliced
curry powder
250 ml coconut milk
2 small chilli peppers, diced
1 clove garlic, finely chopped
lemon juice
salt
oil for frying

1 Boil meat with lemon juice, chilli peppers and salt.

2 Boil green bananas separately.

3 Fry onion until golden, add garlic and curry.

4 Mix with boiled meat and bananas, add coconut milk and cook for a further 15 minutes or until meat is tender.

37

Froga Tal-Chagin (kind of omelette)

125 g cooked spaghetti
2 eggs
30 g grated cheese
parsley, chopped or dried
salt
pepper

1 Beat eggs, season and mix in spaghetti and grated cheese.

2 Cook in oil in frying pan. The omelette should be too thick to be turned in the pan — slide it on to a plate and then back into pan to cook other side.

MEXICO

Piñata

The piñata is one of the favourite games of Mexican children, especially at Christmas and Birthday celebrations.

In Mexico the base of the piñata is a pottery jar of the cheapest kind. However, it may also be made of a paper bag or cardboard box that is easily broken. Piñatas may be made to resemble many different things: toys, people, animals, stars, etc. To create the desired effect, glue to the jar or bag arms, legs, tails, ears, cones, wings, etc, made of such materials as crêpe paper, felt, etc.

The piñata is filled with peanuts, or wrapped candy, and hung on a cord to raise or lower it so that it cannot easily be reached. Players are blindfolded and given a stick approximately a metre (just over 1 yard) long.

The children begin singing the 'piñata song' while the leader turns one child round three times and places her in the centre, touching the piñata with the stick without hitting it, in order to get the feel of where it is. The children continue singing while the piñata is raised and lowered.

Each child tries three times to hit the piñata until one of them breaks it and the contents scatter on the floor. Then all the children run and pick up what they can.

If there is a large group, several piñatas may be used.

Canción de la Piñata

Dale, dale, dale   no pierdas el tino,   mide la dis-

tancia   que hay en el camino

No quiero oro   ni quiero plata

Yo lo que quiero es quebrar la piñata

Guacamole (serves 6)

2 large ripe avocados
2 large tomatoes
60 g onions, chopped
1 clove garlic, chopped fine
coriander leaves, chopped fine
60 ml lime juice
30 ml olive oil
salt and pepper to taste
paprika (optional)

1 Peel and mash avocados and add lime juice immediately (to prevent avocado changing its colour).

2 Mash or chop the tomatoes and add to avocados.

3 Mix in all other ingredients.

Corn Cake

6 or 7 young ears of green corn (or 1 tin sweetcorn)
83 g chopped fruit (oranges, figs, raisins, etc)
4 eggs
milk
1 tbs cream
83 g sugar
140 g flour
125 g melted butter
salt
cinnamon

1 Shake out corn grains and mix together with a little milk. Mix in cream, sugar, butter, salt, flour and beaten eggs.

2 Pour half of this mixture into mould, add a layer of chopped fruit and pour remaining mixture on top.

3 Sprinkle with cinnamon and bake at a low (275°F/150°C) heat for approximately 1 hour.

Alternative Recipe:

For a savoury corn cake with chilli, omit sugar, chopped fruit and cinnamon and add chilli, tomato, garlic and onion.

NETHERLANDS

Erwtensoup (Green Pea Soup)
(serves 6)

675 g smoked sausage
450 g split peas
2 leeks
4 sticks celery
1 bunch parsley
1 bunch celery leaves
2.5 litres water
30 g butter
salt

1 Soak split peas overnight, boil in same water on a very low flame for 2 hours. Salt after one hour.

2 Thinly slice leeks, chop parsley, celery and celery leaves. Fry all vegetables in butter.

3 Add vegetables to peas and continue simmering for 10 minutes.

4 In a separate pan bring water to boil; take off heat and place sausage in it. Leave 15 minutes. Add sausage to soup and cut at table.

NEW ZEALAND

Fire's on Mount Cook (Brownie game)
(Mount Cook is New Zealand's highest mountain.)

Any number can play, indoors or out.

40

Players form a double circle, with the same number in each. 'It' stands in the centre and starts the game by calling out: 'Fire's on Mount Cook, girls, run, run, run!'

Players in the outer circle then run clockwise around the outside of the inner circle. When 'It' calls, 'Fire's out!' each runner must stand in front of a player in the inner circle.

Meanwhile 'It' has already stepped in front of a player. The person left out becomes 'It' in the next round.

Players who ran are now the inner circle, so a different group has a chance to run.

Shopping Basket

Played in Patrols.

Each Patrol takes the 'shopping basket' for about 3 minutes. In the basket are ten packets from the kitchen cupboard, e.g. baking powder, cocoa, soap powder, tea. The girls have a good look at the packets.

Later 20 questions are asked, e.g.: What biscuits are pictured on the cocoa packet? What is the weight on the baking powder packet? Where is the soap made? (The answers should be written down.)

This is a good game for teamwork. The highest scores will come from the Patrols who distributed one or two packets to each member to study.

Wet Day in Camp

Played in Patrols.

The Guider gives each Patrol Leader an envelope. They are told to continue with Patrol Time, and not to open the envelope until the Guider holds up a sign saying 'It's Raining'. When someone in the Patrol sees the sign, they begin.

In each envelope is a card numbered 1 to 6 and six pictures. Pictures are placed on the card in the order in which the Patrol thinks jobs should be done in a sudden shower of rain.

All the Patrols come together to discuss results.

This is good for team work: a Patrol working as a team will allot one job to each Guide, therefore all the jobs will be done at the same time.

41

Waves (Brownie game)

Played in two teams.

Draw two long parallel lines about a metre (just over 1 yard) apart. The two teams stand behind the lines, facing each other. A 'home' must be marked some distance behind one of these lines. Between the lines scatter small stones — the 'shells'.

One team are 'Waves'. They hold hands and swing them backward and forwards while counting loudly 'one, two, three, swish'. The other team are 'Children' picking up shells on the beach. When the Waves shout 'swish' the Children run 'home' while the Waves try to catch them. The ones who are caught join the Waves and the game goes on until all are caught.

The Children count their 'shells' and the teams change over.

Fish Loaf

900 g firm white fish
1 tbs salt
1 tbs cornflour
750 ml boiled milk
60 g melted butter
2 tsp grated nutmeg
pinch pepper

Garnish:

capers
slice of lemon
parsley (optional)

1 Skin, bone and flake fish. Season with salt.

2 Turn into large bowl with cornflour and add milk gradually, mixing well. Add melted butter, nutmeg and pepper.

3 Place mixture in greased pan. Tap sharply to get rid of air bubbles, and bake in slow oven (225-275°F/125-160°C) for 2 hours.

4 Turn loaf out and decorate with capers, lemon and parsley.

PAKISTAN

Mazdoori

This game can be played indoors or out with up to 30 players divided into two equal teams.

Each team chooses a leader, and the teams stand a short distance from each other. The team to start the game is called the Mazdoor (labourers).

The Mazdoor come towards the other team chanting 'If there is some work let us do it; you will never find labourers to compare with us.'

The leader of the other team asks; 'What work can you do?'
The leader of the Mazdoor says, 'We can perform any kind of work.'

The other leader then says, 'All right then, perform your job.'

Mazdoor team members then mime the actions of the Mazdoori (work) they have decided to do. For example, if they are to be carpenters some might saw wood, or use hammers and nails or screwdrivers, etc. If a number of different actions can show different kinds of work involved in a trade, the game becomes more interesting.

The other team has two guesses to discover what kind of work it is. If they guessed correctly, the teams change places.

PAPUA NEW GUINEA

Banana Baki Baki

5 green bananas, I coconut, salt,
green leaves
(fish can be
added if liked)

1 Grate bananas with a shell or a spoon and put in a dish. Cover.

2 Scrape coconut flesh and mix with coconut milk and some water in a saucepan. Bring to boil.

3 When starting to boil, spoon grated banana into the coconut mixture, place fish if used on top and cover with the green leaves. Heat gently until fish is cooked.

Vegetables Cooked in Bamboo

60 g shelled peanuts
4 small sweet potatoes
I slice pumpkin
200 g young green beans
2 medium ripe bananas

(If no bamboo tube is available, make parcels with cooking foil)

1 Roast the peanuts and grind up into flour.

2 Peel, wash and dice sweet potato and pumpkin. Wash and slice beans. Peel and chop bananas.

3 Mix chopped vegetables into peanut flour, and put mixture into a bamboo tube. Add a little water.

4 Close the end of the tube with clean leaves and cook in the fire until the vegetables are soft.

Eggshell Relay

Played in Patrols

Assign a goal or base to each Patrol, and give them each an eggshell and a fan. Each goal must be 2 metres (6'6'') away from the first players. The players should form a single line by Patrols.

The first player of each Patrol holds the fan and the eggshell. When the leader whistles or shouts 'start!' the first player in each Patrol puts the eggshell on the ground and starts fanning, steering the egg to the goal. The egg must not be touched with the fan.

As soon as the eggshell reaches the goal, the player picks it up, runs round the goal and back to the next player.

The next player does the same and so on until the last girl has had her turn. The winners are the Patrol to finish first.

Adobo

450 g pork
450 g chicken
250 ml water

Marinade:

175 ml vinegar
3 tbs oil
1 clove garlic
1 tbs soya sauce
salt
1-2 peppercorns

1 Make marinade with vinegar, oil, soya sauce, garlic, salt and pepper.

2 Cut pork and chicken into cubes and put in marinade for about 1 hour.

3 Put meat and marinade into saucepan, add water and cover. Bring to boil and simmer for 30 minutes.

4 Lower heat and continue simmering until meat is tender and liquid has been absorbed.

Newspaper Walk (Brownie game)

Each Six stands in line, one behind the other, the Sixer standing some distance in front. Each Brownie is given two newspapers on which to step.

When the Sixer blows a whistle the first girl in line passes round her, using the newspapers for each step, and goes back into the line. The second then does the same. This continues until each member of the Six has completed the journey.

The first Six to be standing again in a complete line wins.

Lagan Buri

This game is usually played out of doors in the evening, but can be adapted for indoor or daytime play.

A home base is designated at the beginning of the game, and one player is chosen as 'It'.

She stands away from the other players and from the home base, then throws a handkerchief (lagan) into the air and cries 'buri'. The other players run to find it. No one may run to home base until the handkerchief is found. The player who finds the handkerchief must try to tap the other players before they reach home base. Whoever is tapped is out of the game.

When playing indoors the person who is 'It' may hide the handkerchief instead of tossing it.

SIERRA LEONE

Jollof Rice (serves 8)

I chicken	**1** Cut chicken, beef and bacon into cubes, season, coat with flour and fry in oil until brown. Remove from heat and set aside.
450 g stewing beef	
450 g bacon	
I pack frozen mixed vegetables	
2 onions, sliced	**2** Brown sliced onions in oil, add beef, bacon and tomato paste. Stir well. Simmer with 250 ml water for I hour.
750 g rice	
125 g flour	
I small can tomato paste	**3** Add rest of water and adjust seasoning. Bring to boil, add chicken and rice and simmer until meat is tender and rice is soft.
250 ml cooking oil	
2 litres water	
salt and pepper to taste	
	4 Add vegetables 10 minutes before the end of cooking.

SINGAPORE

Ikan Bilis with Spinach Soup (serves 2)

50 g ikan bilis (sprats/whitebait)	**1** Fry ginger lightly in oil. Add fish and fry for I minute.
250 g spinach, chopped	
I cm piece ginger — chop roughly	**2** Add water, bring to boil and simmer for 10 minutes.
600 ml water	
salt	
vetsin (glutamate)	**3** Add spinach. Cook until tender, season and serve hot.
oil for frying	

Fried Kway Teow (serves 2)

150 g prawns
250 g kway teow (rice noodles)
100 g bean sprouts
1 small piece fish cake, sliced
2 stalks choy sum (chinese kale), chopped
1 egg
2 cloves garlic, finely chopped
1 tsp black sweet sauce
salt, pepper, vetsin (glutamate)
oil for frying

Garnish:

4 red chillies, seeded and sliced

1 Lightly brown garlic in oil.

2 Add choy sum stems and prawns. Fry till cooked, then add bean sprouts, choy sum leaves and fish cake. Stir well, mix in kway teow and seasoning.

3 Push kway teow to the sides of the pan and pour in beaten egg. Stir and mix well.

4 Garnish with chillies and serve hot.

SOUTH AFRICA

Robot game (Brownie game)
Played in teams.

Each group or team is provided with two cards: one with a large red circle on it ('Stop' or 'Wrong'), the other with a large green circle ('Go' or 'Right').

About 12 cards are needed, each with a statement that is either right or wrong e.g. 'Clean water doesn't have bilharzia' (right); 'Don't worry about flies in the city. Only farm flies are dirty' (wrong); 'Dogs can carry worms' (right); 'Wear a hat and a long-sleeved shirt on a hike' (right).

These cards are placed face downwards, one pile for each team. The Brownies in turn pick up a card, read the statement aloud and then put it either with the red or the green circle. The winner is the team with the most correct answers.

Baked Clams

sausagemeat *or* packet of sausages
cheese
tomatoes
onion
bacon

1 Make two long flat cakes with sausagemeat, (if using sausages, skin and use meat).

2 On one cake of sausagemeat layer cheese, tomato, onion and bacon, then top with the other piece.

3 Wrap in heavy foil greased with margarine and bake in hot embers for 20 minutes.

Paxview Special Pudding
(Invented by OFS Guides at Paxview in September 1976)

Biscuits
Custard
Marshmallows
Nuts
Chocolate Chips

1 Line a large flat dish with biscuits.

2 Make a large pot of custard and while hot stir in packet of marshmallows.

3 Pour mixture over biscuits and sprinkle nuts and/or chocolate chips over top. Leave to cool and serve.

SUDAN

The Leopard Trap

Two players make a 'bridge' or 'trap' with their raised arms in the middle of the room. The other players form a large circle and dance round, passing through the trap! The circling players sing a song and clap to its rhythm.

In Sudan the girls sing: 'Lion and leopard, lion and leopard, two night hunters, lion and leopard, lion and leopard, hunt their prey'.

On the last syllable the 'trap' falls, a player is caught and must drop out. The others continue circling and singing, until another player is caught.

The two captured players form another trap.

The game goes on in the same way until only two players remain untrapped — these are the winners.

SWITZERLAND

Käseschnitten nach Trapper-Art
'Hiker's Cheese Slices' (serves 10-20)

20-30 pieces of bread
20 bacon rashers
200 g grated cheese
3-4 eggs
30 ml milk
seasoning

1 Mix cheese, eggs and milk together, season and spread on bread.

2 Lay slices of bacon on top.

3 Cook in moderate (375°F/200°C) oven for 10-15 minutes.

The Giant's House

This game is best played indoors.

Players are divided into teams of 4 or 5; each team chooses a part of the room as a 'team corner'. One person is the game leader.

All the players form a circle, join hands and skip round saying, 'Come inside the giant's house and say what you can see'.
The game leader in the centre says, 'Oh, I can see a snake'. (Or anything else.)

Teams run to their corners and arrange themselves into the shape of a snake or other object named. The team that forms the best shape first gets a point. The game continues as long as the players wish!

The team with most points wins.

Takraw

This game is played with a hollow loosely-woven wicker ball, called a takraw.

Any part of the body, except the hands, can be used to hit the ball, and the object of the game is to keep the ball in the air as long as possible.

There are many variations. The group can stand in a circle and keep score by giving a point to each player who lets the ball touch the ground.

Fruit Salad

bananas
oranges
pineapple
papaya
sugar
condensed milk
pinch of Nescafé

1 Cut bananas, papaya and pineapple into cubes. Peel and slice oranges. Sprinkle with sugar.

2 Mix together with the Nescafé.

3 Serve with condensed milk.

Rainbow Tag (Brownie game)

A box of counters of 3 or 4 different colours is needed, or, if played outdoors, leaves of different shapes or small objects such as twigs, beans and small stones, etc., could be used.

Two Brownies are picked as 'chasers'. Each of the other players has a counter which she holds so that the colour cannot be seen.

The Guiders says 'Go' or blows a whistle and the chasers run after the Pack. Anyone caught must give up her counter; she may then go to the Guider for another one.

The first chaser to have 3 counters of 3 different colours shouts 'stop', and is the winner. Another two chasers are chosen, and the game continues.

Yorkshire Parkin

225 g medium oatmeal
125 g flour
75 g margarine
125 g brown sugar
125 g syrup
125 g treacle
1 egg
125 ml milk
1 tsp ginger and salt

1 Mix oatmeal, flour and ginger in a bowl.

2 Melt margarine, sugar, syrup and treacle together over a low heat. Allow to cool, then mix into dry ingredients.

3 Beat egg and add gradually with milk.

4 Cook for 2 hours in low/medium (235°F/175°C) oven or until firm.

Egg Mornay (A quick recipe for camp supper)

1 egg per person

Cheese sauce:

50 g butter *or* margarine
50 g flour
175 g grated cheese
600 ml milk
seasoning

1 Hard-boil the eggs.

2 Make cheese sauce — melt butter or margarine, blend in flour and gradually mix in milk. Take off the heat, season and add grated cheese. Stir thoroughly until smooth.

3 Pour sauce over eggs, heat through, and serve with crisps (potato chips), salad and/or brown bread and butter.

Bara Brith (Currant or speckled bread)

900 g flour
25 g yeast
225 g brown sugar
225 g butter, margarine or lard

1 Rub fat into flour and add the other dry ingredients.

2 Mix yeast with a little sugar and warm milk.

3 Make a well in the centre and add yeast.

175 g sultanas or raisins
175 g currants
125 g candied peel
1 tsp salt
1 tsp mixed spice
warm milk

Knead into a soft dough. Cover and allow to rise to twice its size in a warm place for about 1 1/2 hours.

4 Turn on to a floured board, put into greased tins and bake in a moderate (375°F/200°C) oven.

5 When cool, slice thinly and butter.

UNITED STATES OF AMERICA

Shape game

Played in pairs.

Two girls sit back-to-back so that neither can see what the other is doing. Each is given the same coloured shapes, which can be made from wood or paper.
One girl makes a design with her shapes and tells the other girl where she is putting each piece. The other girl listens and tries to make the same design.

It is interesting to see how alike or different the designs can be!

Barnyard Bedlam (Brownie game)

Best played outside, in groups.

The Leader hides plenty of pine cones, beans, macaroni pieces or other small objects within a certain area.
Each group chooses an animal name. The Brownies search for the hidden objects, but only one may pick them up. If one of the group finds an object, she makes the noise of the animal her group represents. This calls the Brownie who comes to pick it up. The group which finds the most objects is the winner.

Frog in the Lea (Brownie game)

This game can be played in a large room, play- ground or even shallow water!

Five Brownies are chosen to be 'frogs' and sit cross-legged in a circle, facing out- wards. The rest of the Brownies make a circle round the 'frogs' and skip (if on land) or walk (if in water) repeating, 'Frog in the lea can't catch me!'
The 'frogs' try to touch any Brownie — but without rising or uncrossing their legs! When a Brownie is caught, she changes places with the 'frog' who caught her.

Crab-Clambake (serves 6)

12 small crabs
6 dozen soft-shelled clams
12 small onions
6 medium baking potatoes
6 ears of corn in husks
seasoning

Garnish:

wedges of lemon
butter

1 Wash clams thoroughly.

2 Peel onions and wash potatoes. Parboil for 15 minutes. Drain. Remove corn silk from corn and replace husks.

3 Cut 12 pieces of cheesecloth and 12 pieces of heavy duty aluminium foil 18" x 36" (40 cm x 90 cm) each. Place 2 pieces of cheesecloth on top of 2 pieces of foil, making 6 sets.

4 Place 2 onions, 1 potato, ear of corn, 1 dozen clams and 2 crabs on each of the 6 cheesecloth and foil sets, tie opposite corners together, pour 250 ml water over each package. Bring foil up over the food and close all edges with tight double folds.

5 Place the six packages on a grill about 4" (10 cm) from hot coals. Cover with foil and cook for 45 to 60 minutes or until onions and potatoes are cooked. Serve with butter and lemon wedges.

Olive Halloween Buns

200 g can tuna fish
150 g pitted olives
2 (75 g) packages cream cheese
2 dill pickles, chopped finely
1 green onion, chopped finely
4 tbs mayonnaise
2 tbs milk
4 bread rolls
butter

1 Crumble olives with fingers, then combine with drained, flaked tuna, pickle, onion and mayonnaise.

2 Cut tops off rolls and hollow out centres. Spread insides of rolls with butter. Fill with olive mixture. Replace tops and fasten with toothpicks.

3 Blend together softened cheese and milk. Cover outsides of rolls with cheese.

Chocolate Drop Cookies

215 g oats
350 g sugar
1 tbs cocoa
125 g condensed milk
225 g butter
1 tsp peanut butter
vanilla

1 Put the sugar, milk and cocoa in pan and bring to boil. Boil 1 1/2 minutes.

2 Set aside and blend in butter, oats, peanut butter and vanilla.

3 Drop spoonfuls on greaseproof paper and leave to set.

51

Posole (A recipe inherited from the Arizona Indians)

1.5 kg pork shoulder
1.5 kg canned hominy (a kind of sweet-corn)
2 small onions (chopped)
4 red chilli peppers or 3 tbs chilli powder (less if desired)
1.5 litres water
oregano
crushed clove garlic
salt to taste

1 Place meat and water in saucepan, bring to boil and simmer until meat is tender — about 3 hours

2 Add remaining ingredients and simmer 1/2 to 1 hour longer.

VENEZUELA

Brown and white sandwiches

(Quantities per person)
2 slices brown bread
2 slices white bread
sliced ham
hard boiled egg, sliced
sliced cheese
mayonnaise
butter

Spread mayonnaise on one slice of brown bread. Lay ham on top, followed by one slice of buttered white bread, cheese slice, second slice of brown bread spread with mayonnaise and sliced egg. Finally lay the second slice of white bread on top.

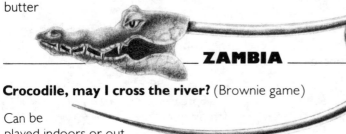

ZAMBIA

Crocodile, may I cross the river? (Brownie game)

Can be played indoors or out.

A line is marked on the ground, and the crocodile (Brown Owl) stands on one side of it facing the Brownies.
The Brownies come to the river bank (the line) chanting: 'Crocodile, crocodile, may I cross your river?' The crocodile answers 'No!'

This is repeated until the crocodile says, 'Yes, if you give me a yellow flower' (or, a safety pin, a stone, anything else which is easily available).

The first Brownie to find whatever is asked for and bring it to the river bank is allowed to cross the river.

The play continues until all the Brownies are across.

Lost Shoe Relay (Brownie game)

Played in Sixes.

The Brownies all take off their shoes and put them in a heap at one end of the room.

They fall in in Sixes and the game is played like an ordinary relay, the Brownies running up to the heaps of shoes, finding their own shoes, putting them on, and running back to their Sixes.

The first Six to finish wins.

Flapjacks

225 g flour
1 1/2 tsp baking powder
salt
water
oil for frying

1 Mix dry ingredients thoroughly with a spoon or peeled stick.

2 Add water slowly, stirring all the time to prevent lumps, to make a thick batter, and leave to stand.

3 In a heavy frying pan heat enough oil to cover bottom. Pour in sufficient batter from the centre to nearly cover bottom of pan and hold the pan over fire, shaking gently to prevent batter sticking. Turn the flapjack and cook the other side.

4 Eat with butter, jam or whatever you like.

Kim's Game

'Kim's Game' is a favourite of Girl Guides/Girl Scouts all over the world. It comes from the story *Kim* by Rudyard Kipling. In the story, Kipling has the game used as an observation exercise for secret service agents in India.

Played in teams. Each team has paper and pencils.

Place 10 to 21 varied objects on a table. All the players study them for two minutes, then the objects should be covered.
Teams make a list of all the objects they remember. The team with the longest correct list wins.

International Kim's Game is a variation of Kim's Game

Played in teams or singly.

Collect sets of postcards, articles, uniform pictures, badges, flags, etc. from many countries. Scatter these round the hall.
Teams have 3-5 minutes discussion time, then each member writes down matching articles, e.g. uniform from Spain, a postcard showing a bull-fight and castanets.

Points are given for finding the most articles about each country, and the team/individual with the most points wins.

GAMES FOR DISABLED (EXTENSION) GUIDES

Most of the games in this book can be adapted to suit every disability. Even if adaptation is not always possible, a disabled girl can be included by, for instance, being given the responsiblity of keeping the score, calling the turns, 'umpiring' the game etc.

Ball games are generally difficult for disabled children because of manipulation and also the frustration of balls rolling away, but can be adapted by the use of bean bags, which are easy to catch and neither bounce nor roll.

Both quiet and noisy games can be enjoyed by Girl Guides/Girl Scouts and Brownies without being labelled 'special', and some games may be useful in helping them to pass tests — imagine the delight of discovering that not only have you had fun, but also you have passed a test in the same way as the others!
The following are a few games which have been used specifically for disabled girls.

Tracking

This can be played in a hall or out-of-doors. Played in Patrols.
One Patrol lays a trail over a given area, using cards with tracking signs on them, stones and twigs. This can lead to 'hidden treasure' — sweets, for instance.

The other Patrols follow the trail by reading the signs. The last patrol collects the stones and twigs.

This game can be played by setting a compass trail, but it should be remembered that wheel chairs can upset the working of a compass.

Pitching

This can be played either in teams or separately.

A large square of cardboard, divided into 6 numbered sections, is placed on the ground. Each girl (or each team) has 6 cardboard discs about 2 1/2" (60 cm) in diameter.

The players in turn position themselves at a suitable distance from the cardboard square according to their ability. They throw the six discs on to the board, scoring points according to which section the discs land on. If a disc lands across a line, the score is based on which section holds the larger part of the disc.

The winner is the team or individual with the highest score.

Shapes or Mixed Bag

Played in Sixes/Patrols.

Each Six or Patrol has a cloth bag, in which are a number of varied articles — but these should be alike both in size and shape. Each bag has the same objects in it.

The Guider calls out the name of an article and the first girl to take that article from her team's bag wins a point.
The bag is passed to the next girl and the game continues until everybody has had a turn.

The Six/Patrol with the most points at the end is the winner.

Note — the time allowed for finding the article in the bag should be very brief!

Battleships and Submarines

Two of the players are chosen as 'battleships'. The rest of the girls are 'submarines'.

The 'battleships' are blindfolded and sit at one end of the room, facing each other, with about a yard (one metre) between them. The 'submarines' start at the other end of the room and must creep up and pass between the 'battleships' without being heard.
If a 'battleship' hears a sound she points directly to it and calls, 'torpedoed!'. If a 'submarine' is there she must sit down on the spot and say, 'sunk!'.

The game continues until all the 'submarines' have been sunk.

Fishing

Played in Sixes or Patrols.

Prepare sets of cards to suit different activities: Compass points, for instance, which should be written on the cards; Rules of Health — pictures to show each one; Knots — drawings or sample knots in coloured cord stuck on the cards. Attach a paper clip to each card.

Each girl has a short stick with a piece of string tied to it and a small magnet on the end of the string.

The cards are scattered on a table — the 'pond'. The game leader calls the topics and the girls 'fish' for the card to match the call.

When all the cards have been 'caught' they are put in order and the girls discuss or otherwise use them as a basis for patrol activity.

_____GAMES FOR THINKING DAY_____

Worldo (Brownie game)

Played in Sixes

Prepare a set of cards for each Brownie with pictures of Brownies from different countries. As many cards as you like may be in a set, but twelve is a good number.

Call out the countries one by one and each girl turns over the appropriate card. The first girl to turn over all her cards calls 'Worldo' and is the winner.

Make the World Go Round!

Place the World Trefoil on a large blank surface with plenty of room all round. The first participant has a look at the location of the Trefoil; is blindfolded; walks a number of paces; then has to place one arrow in an appropriate position. The next participant does the same, until ten girls have tried to form the original Thinking Day symbol. Compete between packs, patrols, etc, to see which can make the best design.

3474/4971A   **02**
SWO#— 179512   PC#—901
CUS#—9105   06/16